Susan Goodman • Sandy Hammer

ACTION BOOKS

FOOD AND DRINK

Published by
New Look Books
PO Box 864
Oxford
OX2 9YD

ISBN 1-901308-03-0

British Library Cataloguing in Publication Data.
A catalogue record for this book is available from the British Library.

Printed and bound in Great Britain.

In the bag

Here's my shopping list. Work out the total cost of my shopping.

cheese £2.20/kg

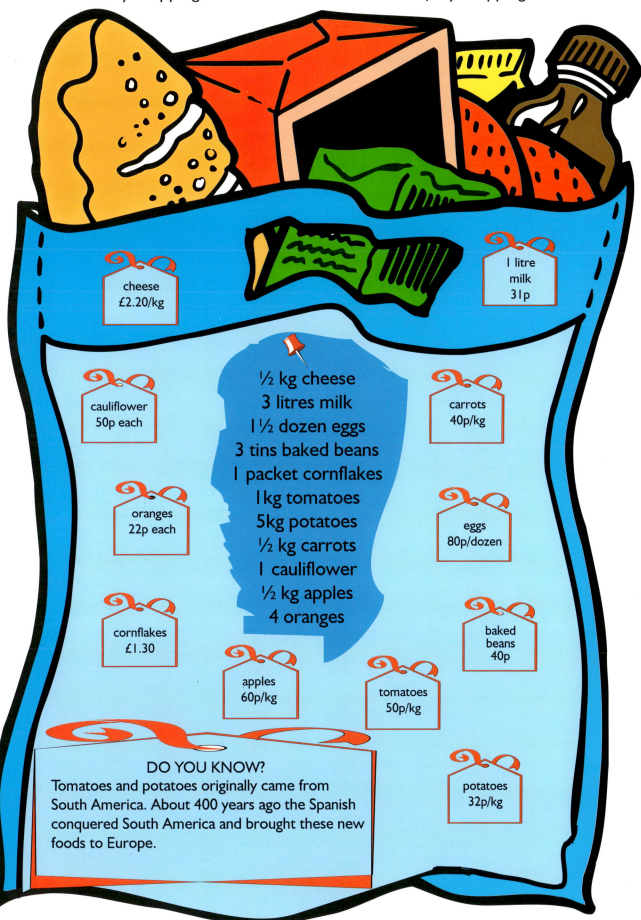

1 litre milk 31p

½ kg cheese
3 litres milk
1½ dozen eggs
3 tins baked beans
1 packet cornflakes
1 kg tomatoes
5kg potatoes
½ kg carrots
1 cauliflower
½ kg apples
4 oranges

cauliflower 50p each

carrots 40p/kg

oranges 22p each

eggs 80p/dozen

cornflakes £1.30

baked beans 40p

apples 60p/kg

tomatoes 50p/kg

potatoes 32p/kg

DO YOU KNOW?
Tomatoes and potatoes originally came from South America. About 400 years ago the Spanish conquered South America and brought these new foods to Europe.

Pasta in a twist

Each of these muddled words is a different type of pasta. Unravel the words and draw the shape of the pasta.

spighetta

raliovi

maconari

salagne

Here is a recipe for a meat sauce to serve with pasta. Make all the measurements metric.

1 oz (ounce) = 28 g
1 teaspoon = 5 ml
1 tablespoon = 15 ml

6 oz lean minced beef
3 oz chopped chicken livers
1 teaspoon dried basil
1 onion chopped
1 x 8 oz tin Italian tomatoes
4 tablespoons tomato puree
1 tablespoon oil

DO YOU KNOW?
The word 'pasta' is Italian for paste, which is made by mixing flour & water together. In Italian spaghetti literally means thin strings; vermicelli, little worms; farfalle, butterflies.

Number noodles

Write the next number in these series.

22	33	44	55	?
123	234	345	456	?
2	5	8	11	?
4	9	16	25	?
67	61	55	49	?
987	876	765	654	?
1	3	9	27	?
64	32	16	8	?
19	28	37	46	?
2	12	72	432	?
272	136	68	34	?
113	311	131	113	?
157	246	335	424	?

Sweet history

Read below about the history of sweets and answer the questions on the next page.

About 2000 years ago Roman children ate sweets, which they bought in confectionery shops. Their sweets were rather different from ours, which are mainly made of sugar. The Romans used honey to provide the sweet flavour.

Romans did have some sugar but it was very expensive. It came from sugar-cane grown in India. This plant is a six-metre high, giant grass with a sugary juice in its stalks. In 1493 Christopher Columbus took sugar-cane plants to the West Indies, where they soon became an important crop. But sugar continued to be an expensive luxury until about 200 years ago, when it was discovered that sugar could be extracted from the root of the sugar-beet plant. This plant can be easily grown even in quite cold places like Britain, unlike sugar-cane which needs a hot, tropical climate.

At about the same time that sugar became cheaper, liquorice sweets were developed. Liquorice is made from the long roots of a plant related to beans. The roots are dug up and dried. The thick liquorice juice, extracted from the roots, is much sweeter than sugar but is unpleasant eaten on its own. The first liquorice sweets were made in 1760 by mixing liquorice, flour, water and sugar.

In this country, children have been able to buy cheap sweets for about 100 years. The sweets have had wonderful names like sherbet dip, bull's-eyes, aniseed balls, liquorice all-sorts, humbugs and gob-stoppers.

True or false

Read the text on the opposite page about the history of sweets and then decide whether these statements are true or false. Tick the box.

	TRUE	FALSE
Roman children ate gob-stoppers.	☐	☐
Romans bought sweets in sweet shops.	☐	☐
Sugar-cane is a large tree.	☐	☐
Columbus lived about 500 years ago.	☐	☐
Sugar-cane contains a sugary liquid.	☐	☐
Sugar-beet grows only in hot countries.	☐	☐
The West Indies have a cold climate.	☐	☐
Liquorice is made from beans.	☐	☐
Bull's-eyes come from animals.	☐	☐

Roman sweets.

Here is a recipe that comes from a Roman cookery book. It was written almost 2000 years ago.

Take the best wheat flour and cook in boiling water or milk until it becomes a stiff paste. Spread onto a plate. When cold, cut up into pieces and fry in the best oil. Remove from the oil and pour honey over them, sprinkle with pepper and serve.

(Don't try this without help from a grown-up.)

Menu maths

Mr. and Mrs. Guzzler took their children Gloria and George out for dinner. They went to the Very Posh Restaurant. Here is the menu.

Menu
Hors d'oeuvres
Fresh melon in white wine £2.50
Tomato soup with croutons £1.50
Entrées
Southern-style chicken £4.80
Beef Stroganoff £6.60
Italian baked fish £3.50
Vegetables
French-fried potatoes £1.20
Cauliflower and herbs £2.30
Garden peas £1.00
Desserts
Ice-cream £2.00
Apple pie £3.20

Mr. Guzzler ordered soup, beef, potatoes, cauliflower, peas, ice-cream.
Mrs. Guzzler ordered the same as Mr. Guzzler but added apple pie as well.
Gloria Guzzler ordered melon, chicken, peas, and five portions of ice-cream.
George Guzzler ordered everything on the menu.

Work out the bill for each Guzzler. Now work out the total cost for the whole family.

A square meal

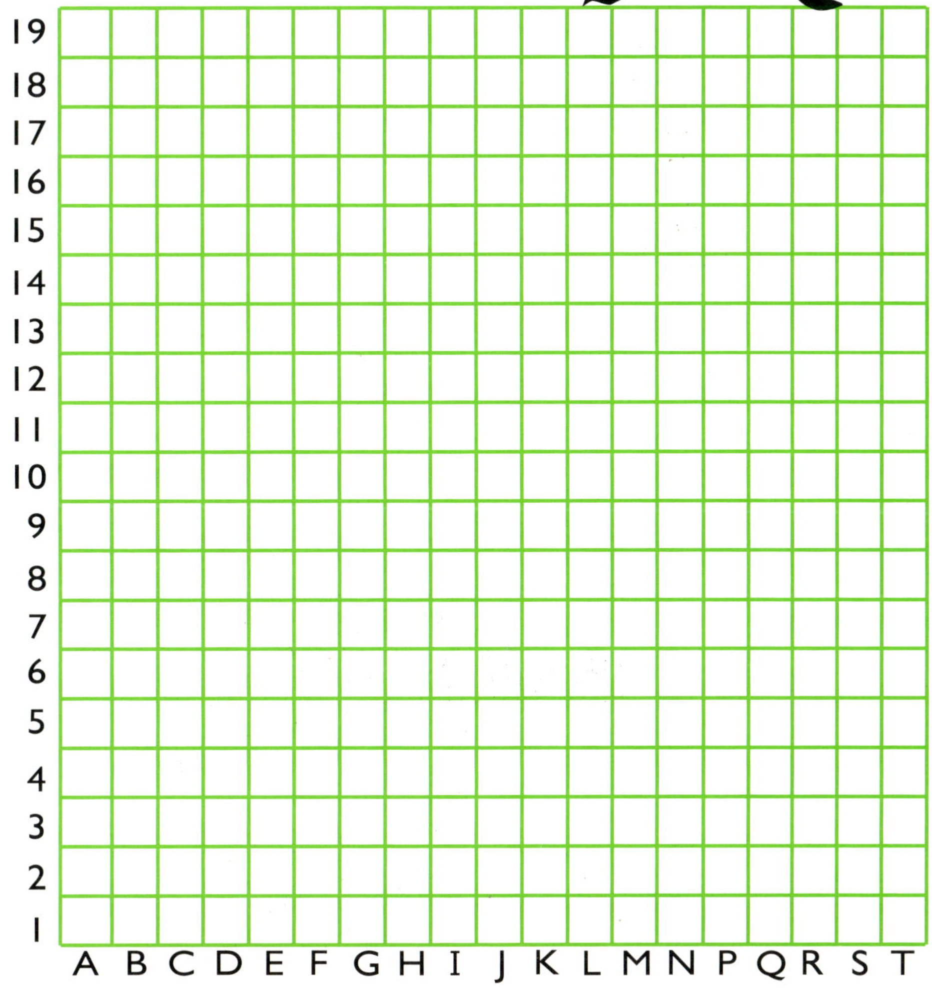

Colour in these squares and find my favorite food.

B2,B3,B4,B5,B6,B9,B10,B11,B12,B13,B15,B16,B17,B18,B19
C4,C6,C9,C13,C17,C19
D4,D5,D6,D9,D13,D19
F2,F3,F4,F5,F6,F9,F10,F11,F12,F13,F15,F16,F17,F18,F19
G2,G4,G6,G11
H2,H6,H9,H10,H11,H12,H13,H15,H17,H18,H19
I15,I17,I19
J2,J3,J4,J5,J6,J9,J10,J11,J12,J13,J15,J16,J17,J19
K4,K6
L2,L3,L4,L5,L6,L9,L10,L11,L12,L13,L15,L16,L17,L18,L19
M11,M13,M17
N2,N4,N5,N6,N11,N12,N13,N15,N16,N17,N18,N19
P2,P4,P6
Q2,Q3,Q4,Q6,Q9,Q11,Q12,Q13
R9,R11,R13
S9,S10,S11,S13

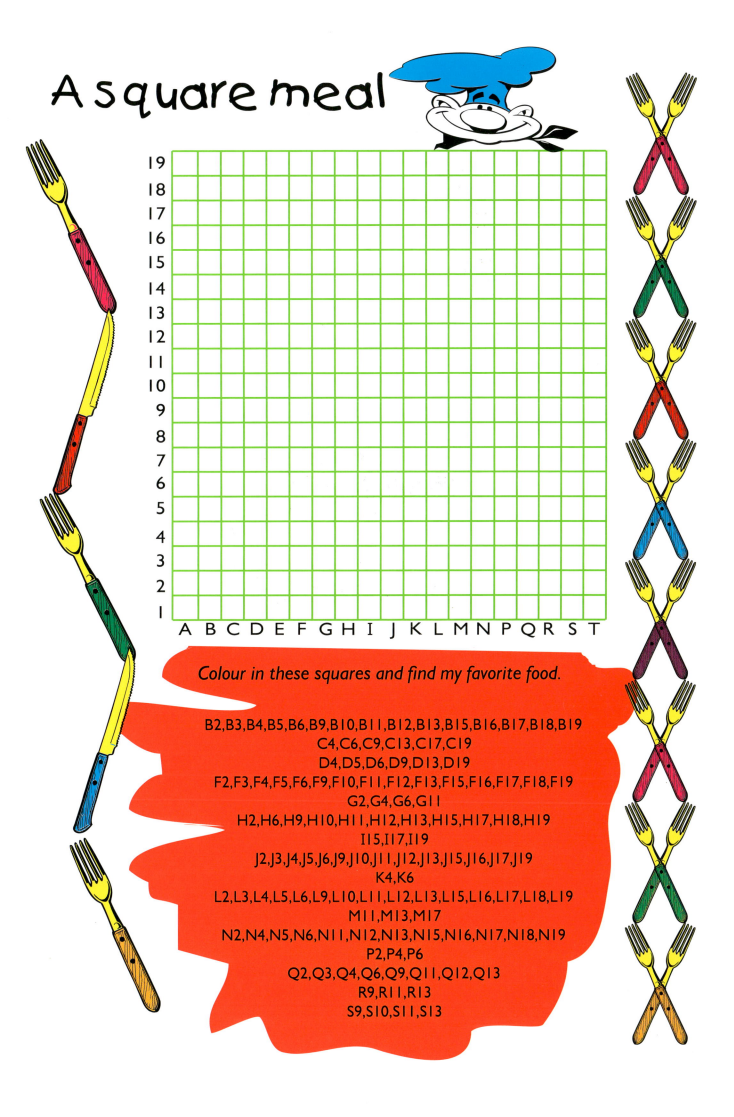

Fish scales

Mr. Guzzler buys 1.5kg of sardines. There are 12 sardines in a kg. How many sardines does he buy?

Mrs. Guzzler buys 1kg of a small fish called whitebait. About 20 whitebait weigh 50g. How many whitebait does she buy?

The Guzzler children buy 120 sprats. There are about 30 per kg. What weight of fish did they buy?

The Guzzlers are holding a party for 120 people. Each person will be given a trout and salad to eat. One trout weighs 0.5kg and costs £2. How much is the total trout bill for the party?

DO YOU KNOW?
The Japanese eat more fish per person than any other nation. They catch about 122 million tonnes a year. That's enough to provide 100kg of fish a year for every man, woman and child in Japan.

Fish fun

*Here is a list of some common edible fish.
Rewrite it in alphabetical order.*

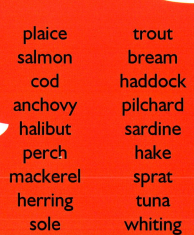

plaice
salmon
cod
anchovy
halibut
perch
mackerel
herring
sole
trout
bream
haddock
pilchard
sardine
hake
sprat
tuna
whiting

In the paragraph below cross out the words spelt wrongly.

In many parts of the world fish farms are (maid, made) by fencing off parts of the sea along the coast. (Hear, Here) sea-water fish are (bred, bread). Shrimp, crabs and lobsters are also (groan, grown). In farms (their, there) is protection from predators, and of (cause, course) it is easier to bring in the catch.

Find how many words can you make from the word

Fishmonger

15:good
20:very good
25:excellent

DO YOU KNOW?
Most of the world's fish are caught in the deep oceans. The deep-sea fishing fleets are too far from land to bring their catch back the same day. They stay at sea for weeks or months passing their catches into a 'factory ship'. Here the fish are cleaned, gutted and frozen.

Mythical apples

In ancient Greek myths, golden apples were regarded as a special prize. The strongest man in the world, Herakles (known as Hercules in Latin), risked his life to pick twelve golden apples. In the myth told below, three goddesses enter a beauty competition for the prize of a golden apple. But the award of this prize brought disaster on earth.

One day the Greek gods were enjoying a wonderful party when suddenly a trouble-making goddess, called Eris, threw a golden apple among the guests. On the apple were the words 'for the fairest'. Three goddesses immediately claimed the apple. Someone would have to choose between these proud, godly beauties.

The king of the gods, Zeus, decided that a young man, Paris, Prince of Troy, should make the choice. What a difficult decision! Each goddess revealed to him her divine beauty and each offered him a bribe. Hera promised him power if he chose her. Athena offered him wisdom. And Aphrodite promised him Helen, the most beautiful woman in the world, as his wife.

Paris chose Aphrodite. Of course the two rejected goddesses were very upset and became bitter enemies of Paris.

Unfortunately the promised Helen was already married, to a king of Greece. Paris rushed off, kidnapped her and escaped, taking the lovely Helen back to Troy. But the rejected goddesses got their revenge: for ten years war raged between Troy and Greece. Troy was destroyed and Paris killed.

From the group of words below underline those which best describe how both Hera and Athena felt after Paris had made his choice.

worried	jealous	delighted	resentful
relieved	bitter	happy	pleased
joyful	angry	rejected	flattered

Put letters in the empty brackets so that they end the first word and also start the second word. The new words are closely linked with the above story.

Example: gold (e n) joy

rage (_) read
goddess (_ _) cape
no (_) inner
he (_) age
part (_) ears

Cheese please 

Use this code to find the names of the different cheeses.

A B C D E F G H I J K L M N O P Q R S T U V W X Y Z
Y Z A B C D E F G H I J K L M N O P Q R S T U V W X

AFCBBYP

AFCQFGPC

AYKCKZCPR

ZPGC

CBYK

EMSBY

QRGJRML

NYPKCQYL

Now decode this fact.

NYPKCQYL GQ JCDR SN RM
RFPCC WCYPQ ZCDMPC GR GQ
PCYBW RM CYR

CHEESE-MAKING

Here's a way to see what happens in cheese-making. You must get a grown-up to help you. Add lemon juice or vinegar to milk, and heat in a pan. Small solid bits form called 'curds'. The liquid part is called the 'whey'. Cheese is made by heating and pressing the curds into moulds and leaving to mature. In some cheeses with blue streaks (called 'veins') moulds are added.

In real cheese-making the curds are formed by adding a substance called 'rennet' to the milk. Rennet is taken from the stomach juices of young calves.

Good health

To stay healthy we must eat a wide range of foods. They provide our bodies with essential chemicals called 'nutrients'. Each nutrient has a particular job in the body. For example, proteins are the main bodybuilders; fats are important for energy; calcium helps bones to grow properly.

Cheese is an especially nutritious food. Most cheeses have a high fat content of about 50 per cent. They are also a good source of protein and calcium, as well as lots of vitamins including A, D, E and the B complex.

This chart shows the amount of protein and calcium in cheese and some other common foods.

	protein g	calcium mg
2 slices bread	9	100
glass of milk	6	220
60g cheese (about 3 slices)	14	460
2 eggs	20	100
100g potatoes (one small potato)	2	8

A child 9-10 years old needs 28g protein and 550mg calcium every day.

Two of these meals each provide all the protein and calcium a 9 year-old needs in a day. Which meals are they?

a. 6 potatoes, 2 slices of bread, 2 eggs.
b. 2 eggs, 3 slices of cheese.
c. 3 potatoes, 2 eggs, 1 glass of milk.
d. 2 glasses of milk, 2 slices of bread, 2 slices of cheese.

Meaty morsels

Join the animal with the name of its meat.

venison beef pork
cow veal
pig mutton sheep
deer calf

Spell check

There are 8 words spelt wrongly in the following passage. Underline the words and rewrite them correctly.

Meat is the flesh of annimals. It is made up of muscle. In old animales and those wich have had a lot of exercise the mussel becomes thik and tuff. The meet is then difficult to eat and has to be cooked sloly to make it tender.

DO YOU KNOW?

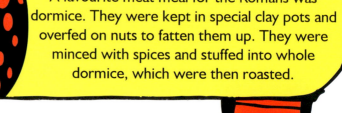

A favourite meat meal for the Romans was dormice. They were kept in special clay pots and overfed on nuts to fatten them up. They were minced with spices and stuffed into whole dormice, which were then roasted.

Beefy riddles

Find the letters and solve the puzzles.

What am I?

my first is in **bend** but not in **sent**
my second is in **sun** but not in **tent**
my third is in **ran** but not in **band**
my fourth is in **gas** but not in **sand**
my fifth is in **idea** but not in **paid**
my sixth is in **radio** but not in **made**
my whole is a quick beefy meal

my first is in **last** but not in **tell**
my second is in **belt** but not in **bell**
my third is in **lace** but not in **coal**
my fourth is in **cape** but not in **pole**
my fifth is in **leak** but not in **leaf**
my whole is a thick juicy slice of beef

Letter play

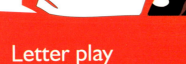

This puzzle has nothing to do with the meaning of the words. Underline the correct word in the brackets. (Look at the letter order.)

Example: meat is to tame as team is to (meat, **mate,** meet)

meat is to tame as leap is to (peal, pale, peel)
lamb is to malt as rose is to (rest, sort, star)
veal is to love as rent is to (rave, tore, rove)
calf is to face as ream is to (race, mere, meet)
beef is to beet as case is to (cart, cast, cake)

Pop puzzle

Cross out all the letters which appear more than once. The letters left spell a favourite drink.

M	K	P	A	B	E
R	L	T	I	F	N
N	I	F	S	H	P
E	B	C	E	D	M
I	S	M	K	R	T
D	R	H	B	O	H

Party time!

It's party time and we must work out how much lemonade, cherryade, orangeade and cola we need to buy.

There will be 20 people at the party. Each will drink on average two glasses of pop. Each glass holds 500ml. How many litres will be drunk?

If the same amount of each type of drink is drunk, how many litres of each are needed?

Shake up

Join each pair of letters to a three-letter word and so make new words that are to do with drinks.

gl gr st dr fl ju

ask ape ass ice ink raw

Milkshake

Solve the multiplication problems in the glasses. Use each answer to find a letter from the code. Rearrange the letters in each row to make the name of a product made from milk.

M	H	Y	R	U	T	B	C	G	A	E	O	S
14	15	16	18	20	24	27	28	30	32	36	49	72

DO YOU KNOW?
Most milk drunk in the world comes from cows. But milk can also be taken from sheep, goats, camels, yaks, buffalo and reindeer.

Giant wordsearch

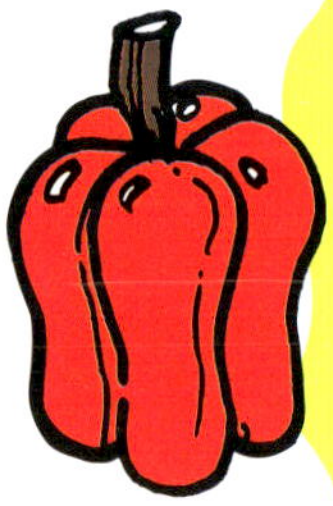

G	M	O	A	I	E	F	U	O	K	R	A	R	W
O	D	E	P	O	T	A	T	O	N	P	K	E	Y
C	P	N	L	G	V	D	S	D	A	I	M	L	R
A	F	S	E	O	C	H	E	R	R	Y	O	I	R
B	O	B	E	A	N	X	M	V	O	I	R	N	E
B	T	Y	K	R	H	U	B	A	R	B	A	F	B
A	A	E	O	H	C	A	E	P	E	D	E	O	W
G	M	L	V	Y	N	R	H	C	X	T	P	R	A
E	O	P	C	A	U	L	I	F	L	O	W	E	R
E	T	P	N	T	F	M	U	L	H	R	N	P	T
D	H	A	L	S	D	E	G	N	A	R	O	P	S
E	M	O	D	U	K	R	I	D	V	A	M	E	U
W	O	J	T	W	M	A	F	R	I	C	E	P	B
S	G	R	A	P	E	C	U	T	T	E	L	S	A

Go forwards, backwards, up, down, and diagonally.
Find all these words:

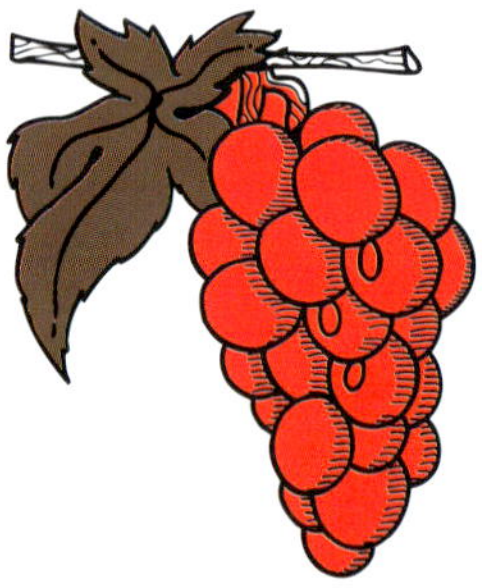

- banana
- cherry
- apple
- cauliflower
- rhubarb
- date
- onion
- tomato
- okra

- carrot
- pear
- strawberry
- orange
- fig
- lemon
- cabbage
- plum
- melon

- peach
- bean
- pea
- grape
- leek
- swede
- pepper
- lettuce
- potato

Fruity fling

All the answers below are types of fruit. When the puzzle is completed you will find a word going down in the yellow boxes. The word belongs in this sentence:

'A carefully arranged bowl of fruit is most _ _ _ _ _ _ _ _ _'

grows in hands and bunches

rhymes with rare

grows on a vine

yellow and sour

mix red and yellow

used in cider

same name as a New Zealand bird

Honeydew is one type

rhymes with tango

DO YOU KNOW?

The word orange comes from the Arabic *naranj*. Oranges probably first grew in China and were brought by Arabs to India, the Middle East and then Europe. Oranges have been grown in Italy and southern France for almost 1000 years.

ANSWERS

In the bag

Here is the cost of each item in the shopping-list order:
£1.10, 93p, £1.20, £1.20 £1.30, 50p
£1.60, 20p 50p, 30p, 88p.
Total cost: £9.71

Pasta in a twist

spaghetti, ravioli, macaroni, lasagne.
Metric recipe in list order:
168g, 84g, 5ml, 224g, 60ml, 15ml.

Number noodles

66, 567, 14, 36, 43, 543, 81, 4, 55, 2592, 17, 311, 513

Sweet history

False, True, False, True, True, False,
False, False, True and False (depending on whether they are sweets or real eyes).

Menu maths

Mr Guzzler: £14.60
Mrs Guzzler: £17.80
Gloria: £18.30
George: £28.60
Total: £79.30

A square meal

FISH PEAS CHIPS

Fish scales

18 sardines, 400 whitebait, 4kg sprats, £240.

ANSWERS

Fish fun
made, here, bred, grown, there, course.

Mythical apples
jealous, resentful, bitter, angry, rejected.
d, es, w, r, y.

Cheese please
Going down the first column; CHEDDAR, CHESHIRE, CAMEMBERT, BRIE. Going down the second column; EDAM, GOUDA, STILTON, PARMESAN.
PARMESAN IS LEFT UP TO THREE YEARS BEFORE IT IS READY TO EAT.

Good health
b and d.

Meaty morsels
deer, venison; cow, beef; pig, pork; calf, veal; sheep, mutton.
animals, animals, which, muscle, thick, tough, meat, slowly.

Beefy riddles
burger, steak, pale, sort, tore, mere, cast.

Pop puzzle
cola, 20 litres drunk, 5 litres.
glass, grape, straw, drink, flask, juice.

Milkshake
cream, cheese, butter, yoghurt.

Fruity fling
banana, pear, grape, lemon, orange, apple, kiwi,
melon, mango. APPEALING

CLUES

In the bag
You may use a calculator.

Pasta in a twist
It's not difficult to guess most of the pasta names but you may check the spelling in a dictionary.

Number noodles
Here are some clues to the ways the series are made:

a) adding on the same number.
c) taking away the same number.
d) halving each number.
e) look for simple patterns e.g. 123 becomes 312 if you move the last number to the beginning.
f) in three figure numbers look how each digit changes.

Menu maths
You may use a calculator.

Fish scales
1.5 is the same as one and a half
1000g = 1kg
Work out how many whitebait in 100g first. The weight of the trout is not important.

Cheese please
Notice that the code letters are the bottom row of the two alphabets. So CBYK becomes EDAM.

Good health
Work out carefully the protein for each meal. Note that the amount in the chart for cheese is for 3 slices, 2 slices is about 9g of protein. Now find out which have enough calcium.

Beefy riddles
meat and tame:
the letters of the second word contains all the letters of the first word but in a different order.
lamb and malt:
'l', 'a', 'm' of 'lamb' are rearranged to give 'm', 'a', 'l' and a final 't' is added.
veal and love:
the second letter of the second word has become 'o'. 'v', 'e' and 'l' have changed their positions.
calf and face:
the last letter of 'calf' is the first in 'face'. 'a' is in the same place. The first letter in 'calf' is the third in 'face'. The second word has an 'e' added.

Pop puzzle
Two glasses of 500ml = 1000ml = 1 litre.

Milkshake
Make sure you know your tables.